DATE DUE

MARTIAL ARTS

MARTIAL ARTS: PERSONAL DEVELOPMENT

BRYANT LLOYD

The Rourke Press, Inc.
Vero Beach, Florida 32964

Consultant for this series: Michael T. Neil, master instructor of Korean Martial Arts; head instructor of Mike Neil's Traditional Martial Arts Centers, Batavia, IL.

EDITORIAL SERVICES:
Penworthy Learning Systems

Library of Congress Cataloging-in-Publication Data

Lloyd, Bryant. 1942-
    Martial arts—personal development / Bryant Lloyd.
        p. cm. — (Martial arts)
    Includes index.
    Summary: Discusses briefly some of the personal and social benefits of studying the martial arts including development of discipline, self-esteem, humility, courage, and respect for others.
    ISBN 1-57103-229-0
    1. Martial arts—Psychological aspects—Juvenile literature. 2. Martial arts—Moral and ethical aspects—Juvenile literature. [1. Martial arts—Psychological aspects. 2. Martial arts—Moral and ethical aspects.]
    I. Title II. Series: Lloyd, Bryant. 1942- Martial arts.
    GV1102.7.P75L56 1998
    796.8—dc21   98–22413
                                                                     CIP
                                                                      AC

Printed in the USA

TABLE OF CONTENTS

PERSONAL DEVELOPMENT

When you think **martial arts** (MAHR shul AHRTS), you think of self-defense. You imagine quick hands and flying feet.

Martial arts do develop your physical skills. But martial arts are not just for physical well-being.

At least in **traditional** (truh DISH uh nul) martial arts, the training that makes you stronger physically can also help your personal growth. Part of traditional martial arts training is to make good citizens as well as good martial artists.

Each of the martial arts systems has its own advantages. One is not better than another.

Flying feet and excellence in self-defense are only parts of a well-rounded martial arts training program.

CITIZENSHIP

Being a good citizen means giving to **society** (suh SI uh tee) as well as taking from it. It means trying to make a difference, trying to make the home, neighborhood, town, and country better places for everyone.

Martial arts team practices for its appearance at a fund-raising event.

Most instructors encourage citizenship in their students.

Many martial arts instructors are strong voices for good **citizenship** (SIT uh zen ship). They encourage their students to work in fund-raising programs. Sometimes, for example, a team of martial arts students can earn money for charity by demonstrating their skills.

VALUES

Being a good citizen means having high ideals, or values. Martial arts training often helps promote those ideals.

Martial arts instructors in traditional arts support such values as these: courage, humility, respect, discipline, self-control, and **self-esteem** (SELF es TEEM). These ideals can carry over from the martial arts training room to every part of a student's life.

Martial arts training helps its students gain experience with these ideals. Over time, each young martial artist can develop a strong set of personal values.

Martial arts instructors help students learn values as well as techniques of the art.

RESPECT

Martial arts students work closely with people who may be different from them. Respect gives value to people who may be different from you. Respect for each other is a big part of traditional martial arts training.

In martial arts, handshakes, bows, and courtesy—"Yes, sir," "no, ma'am"—are traditional. Eventually, these signs of respect help root genuine respect for others in students. Respect becomes part of the martial artist's makeup.

The actual beginning of karate is a mystery. One legend suggests that Ta Mo, a Buddhist monk, began the art nearly 1,500 years ago.

Martial artists learn to respect people who are different from them.

DISCIPLINE

Learning martial arts depends upon discipline. Discipline is more than an instructor giving orders and a class obeying. Being disciplined means you're closing the distance between what you're doing and what you should be doing. It means knowing what's right and doing it—without having to be told to do it.

A martial arts instructor helps students teach themselves to be disciplined.

Discipline in training helps this martial arts student break a pine board.

At this point, the martial arts student has become self-disciplined. He or she has taken on the responsibility of doing something without being told to do it.

SELF-ESTEEM

Look into the mirror, even into your heart. Do you like what you see? Martial arts training can help you feel better about yourself. It can build your sense of worth, or self-esteem.

The success you can achieve in martial arts supports a sense of value about yourself. Martial arts training works on your self-esteem through good works.

In the mid-1900s, several Korean martial arts styles were blended together. These styles, known as "kwans," became tae kwon do.

Self-esteem—feeling good about yourself—is a benefit of martial arts.

HONESTY

Honesty of course, requires being truthful. In martial arts, real honesty goes beyond telling the truth.

Honesty means being truthful to yourself as well as to others. It means that you avoid the popular values around you if they are not *your* values. It means being honest about your efforts to learn and exercise. It requires that you ask yourself, "Am I making as great an effort as I can? Am I being all that I can be?"

Martial arts require an honest effort.

17

COURAGE

Students in martial arts know some things about courage. Courage is showing bravery, "guts"—and more. It means standing up for what's right, even if it is not a popular stand.

Determination in martial arts training builds character as well as fitness.

The physical contact of martial arts requires courage.

Courage is never easy. But it is part of what makes a good martial arts student and a good citizen.

Martial arts students show courage and determination in their attention to training. They also show courage by going to the assistance of others.

CHARACTER

What kind of person are you? Are you of good character?

Martial arts training helps build all-around good character. It teaches you how to deal with other people in a correct, honest way.

Traditional martial arts, like tang soo do, teach the values outlined in this book. Good character shows in your **behavior** (be HAYV yer)—how you act. Martial artists are not trained to be bad actors.

Many differences exist within one type of martial art, such as karate. Those differences make it difficult to have competitions between schools.

Martial artists show good manners—and good character—after the competition as well as during it.

GLOSSARY

behavior (be HAYV yer) — the way a person acts

citizenship (SIT uh zen ship) — the state of holding membership in a community

martial arts (MAHR shul AHRTS) — the many systems of fighting, or combat, using mainly the hands and feet

self-esteem (SELF es TEEM) — the value that a person places on him- or herself; the way you see yourself

society (suh SI uh tee) — the larger community of people around you, with whom you share certain values and ideals

traditional (truh DISH uh nul) — that which is done now in the same way that it has always been done

One-on-one teaching helps martial arts students in their personal as well as physical development.

INDEX

FURTHER READING

Find out more about martial arts with these helpful books and information sites:

Armentrout, David. *Martial Arts.* Rourke, 1997.

Blot, Pierre. *Karate for Beginners.* Sterling, 1996.

Potts, Steve. *Learning Martial Arts.* Capstone, 1996.

American Judo and Jujitsu Federation online at—http://www.ajjf.org/ajjf.html

Martial Arts Menu page online at—
  http://www.mindspring.com/~mamcgee/martial.arts./htm/

Martial Arts Resource page online at—
  http://www.middlebury.edu/~jswan/martial.arts/ma.html

Shotokan Karate International (SKIF) USA Headquarters online at—
  http://www.csun.edu/~hbcsc302/